Reversal of Development in Argentina

Reversal of Development in Argentina
Postwar Counterrevolutionary Policies and Their Structural Consequences

Carlos H. Waisman

Princeton University Press

Princeton, New Jersey

To my parents

Contents

List of Tables / ix
Preface / xi

1. **The Argentine Riddle and Sociology of Development / 3**
   The Argentine Question / 3
   *The Breakdown of the International Order and Its
   Consequences / 12*
   Argentina and Social Theory / 18

2. **Is Argentina a Deviant Case? Resource Endowments,
   Development, and Democracy in Sociological Theory / 24**
   *The Classification of Societies in Adam Smith and
   Tocqueville / 25*
   The Classification of Societies in Marx and Engels / 27
   *The Classification of Societies in Turner and the Staple
   Theorists / 31*
   Two Models and the Argentine Case / 33

3. **Images and Facts: Argentina Against the New Country
   and Latin American Mirrors / 36**
   Images. New Country or Underdeveloped Society? / 36
   *Argentine Land and Labor Endowments in a
   Comparative Perspective / 51*
   Overview of the Reversal: Economy and Society / 58
   Overview of the Reversal: Society and Politics / 77

4. **In Search of Argentina: The Adequacy of Various Factors
   for the Explanation of the Reversal / 94**
   The Cultural Factor / 95
   Economic and Social Hypotheses / 106
   The Institutionalization of Ungovernability / 117

5.   **Why the State Became Autonomous in the Forties / 128**
      The Shift in Industrial and Labor Policies / 130
      Ruling Class Interests and External Determinants / 137
      The Autonomy of the State: "Eastern" Society and
      Vertical Cleavage Hypotheses / 143
      The Autonomy of the State: The External Constraint
      Factor / 149
      The Autonomy of the State: The Elite Fragmentation
      Factor / 155
      The Resolution of the Crisis / 158
      Conclusion / 162

      The Primacy of Politics:
      The Question of Revolution in the Forties / 164
      Political Entrepreneurship and the Rhetorical Use of
      Economic Policy: Protectionism as an Antidote to
      Revolution / 164
      Responses by Upper Classes and State Elites:
      Instrumental versus Ideological Interests / 173
      How Realistic was the Fear of Revolution? / 190

7.   **Social Integration and the Inordinate Fear of**
      Communism / 206
      The Cognitive Dimension of Elite Strategies / 209
      Threats from Below: The Image of a Dangerous Working
      Class / 211
      Models from Without: The Logic of International
      Demonstration Effects / 229
      The Argentine Paradox / 250

8.   **The Disadvantages of Modernity / 253**
      A Recapitulation: The Argentine Question Reconsidered
      / 253
      Theoretical Implications / 264
      Epilogue: How the Counterrevolutionary Policies of the
      Forties Generated the Revolutionary Situation in the
      Seventies / 277

      Bibliography / 287
      Index / 319

List of Tables

1.1   Ratios of the Argentine per Capita Product to that of Other Selected Countries, 1913–82 / 6

2.1   Types of Non-Core Agrarian Society / 34

3.1   Agricultural Density, Farm Size, and Land Tenure in Selected Countries around the Time of the Argentine Reversal / 52

3.2   Agricultural Yields before and after the Argentine Reversal / 59

3.3   Agriculture and Industry in Selected Countries during and after the Argentine Reversal / 60

3.4   Net Value of Manufacturing Production per Capita before and after the Argentine Reversal / 62

3.5   Standards of Living in Argentina and in Selected Countries / 73

3.6   Higher Education in Argentina and in Selected Countries / 74

6.1   Industrial Employment in Manufacturing According to Its Vulnerability to the Resumption of Imports, Argentina, 1944 / 202

Preface

This book is a sociological interpretation of the reversal of economic and political development in Argentina. It focuses on the question of why Argentina became an underdeveloped society. This country was not always a part of the underdeveloped periphery: it is more properly an impoverished "new country," or "land of recent settlement."

My argument focuses on the issue of revolution. The reversal of Argentine development was the unintended consequence of policies carried out by the state in the forties, and one of the central justifications for these policies was that they would prevent a revolution in the postwar period. Paradoxically, if the economic progress and political liberalization of Argentina were a direct consequence of the Industrial Revolution in England, the country's stagnation and political crisis were, to a considerable extent, a delayed result of the reaction to the Russian revolution.

Further, I assert that there was no actual revolutionary danger, that a sector of the state elite panicked as a consequence of distorted political knowledge, and that these policies had the effects they did precisely because of the "modern" characteristics of the Argentine social structure, those which set the country apart from the underdeveloped nations.

I focus on the thirties and forties because this was the period in which Argentina switched developmental tracks and became an underdeveloped society. In future publications, I intend to discuss economic and political processes in the seventies. The upheaval and reaction that characterized that decade, the next turning point in Argentine history, were the aftermath of choices made by a sector of the elite in the forties.

In this book I discuss some aspects of Argentine history, but it is not a continuous or systematic historical account. The argu-

ment moves back and forth between historical description and sociological analysis. My goal is to propose an interpretation of
known facts, rather than to discover unknown ones. In the tradition of comparative historical sociology, I make use of the evi-
dence collected by historians and social scientists, and also of sta-
tistics, government documents, and intellectuals' works, in order
to answer a question derived from the sociological theory of development.

Chapter 1 presents the problem posed by Argentina's curvilinear pattern of development. Chapter 2 shows that Argentina is a
deviant case from the point of view of social theory. Since most
readers of this book are likely to have a limited knowledge of the
country, I summarize the various images of Argentina, the peculiarities of the country's social structure, and the main traits of its
economic and political development in Chapter 3. Chapter 4 dis-
cusses different interpretations of the reversal of development.
The causes of the autonomy of the state in the forties are analyzed
in Chapter 5. Chapter 6 deals with the question of revolution in
the forties. Chapter 7 focuses on the cognitive dimension of elite
strategies. Finally, Chapter 8 recapitulates the argument, and dis-
cusses the theoretical implications of the Argentine case.

In this book, I refrained from coining new terms or redefining
old ones, something I did in *Modernization and the Working
Class*. However, I use three words with the specific meaning they
have in Argentine politics. They are liberalism, nationalism, and
oligarchy. Liberalism is used always in the traditional Lockean
sense. When referring to economic policy, it means laissez-faire
economics. Economic and political liberalism do not necessarily
imply each other: since the Depression, most Argentine supporters of economic liberalism have backed political authoritarianism. Nationalism in Argentina is a right-wing authoritarian political ideology, and most left-wing nationalists avoid the label.
Oligarchy, finally, refers to the agrarian elite that ruled the country until the forties. As for general concepts, the only other speci-
fication that should be mentioned is that I always use the term
corporatism in the sense of state or inclusionary corporatism.

The research leading to this book began in the academic year
1978/79, most of which I spent in Buenos Aires. This was a strange
hour in Argentine history. The country was under the control of
an array of eccentrics whose respect for human life was unusually
limited. A few Argentines resisted, usually in simple but still
meaningful ways; many tried to disconnect themselves from the

bizarre context in which they lived; and most adapted to it, by practicing denial, compensation, and rationalization on a large scale. That year, I learned a great deal about the plasticity of human nature, but I felt often uneasy and sometimes guilty for devoting my time to an activity such as research, which appeared irrelevant and even frivolous at that time and place.

I gratefully acknowledge the support given to me by several organizations and individuals during my involvement with this project. In 1978/79, I was a visiting researcher at the Instituto Torcuato Di Tella, in Buenos Aires. I worked at the Central Bank Library and other specialized libraries. Several persons facilitated my work in that period. Torcuato S. Di Tella put at my disposal a collection of lectures on industrial policy published by the Unión Industrial Argentina in the early forties. For the past years, the two of us were working on books on different topics (his is the just published *Sociología de los procesos políticos*), but we were both interested in such phenomena as the impact of mass immigration on the nature of the Argentine political system in the beginning of the century, and the fears felt by the Argentine elites in the postwar period. Our views converged on the first of these issues, and were slightly different on the second. Javier Villanueva, the foremost student of Argentine economic policies in the forties, was kind enough to share with me his knowledge of the issues and the sources. Vicente Pellegrini of the Centro de Investigación y Acción Social provided me with a crucial document of the National Postwar Council in his possession. I completed the final revision of the manuscript in 1985–86, while I was embarked on a new project. I spent the year doing research at the Hoover Library, Stanford University, supported by a National Fellowship from the Hoover Institution and by funds from the University of California, San Diego. My travel and the typing of the manuscript were made possible by grants from the Academic Senate of the University of California, San Diego.

Gino Germani and Miguel Murmis introduced me first to the peculiarities of the Argentine social structure, and my understanding of the Argentine economy was shaped by the work of Carlos F. Díaz Alejandro. During these years, my encounters with Miguel Murmis were infrequent but always rewarding. Gino Germani died when I was beginning my research, and Carlos Díaz Alejandro died when the first draft of the manuscript was completed. I would have very much liked to discuss the book with them. During my work on the project, I benefited from the criticism and advice of many people. I had stimulating conversations about the topic of this book with Darío Cantón, David and Ruth Collier, Marcelo Diamand, Shmuel Eisenstadt, Seymour Martin Lipset, Tim McDaniel, Carlos Moyano Llerena, José E. Miguens, Miguel Murmis, Robert Packenham, James Petras, Alejandro Portes, Robert Wesson, and a long list of colleagues at the University of California, San Diego. I received written comments from Juan Corradi, Paul W. Drake, Lewis Gann, Peter Gourevitch, David Rock, Ramón E. Ruiz, and Michael Schudson. I thank all these people, and I relieve them from any responsibility for the errors of fact or interpretation this work may contain. I am also grateful to Sandra Robertson and Brad Westbrook, who contributed their editorial abilities to different parts of the manuscript, and to Irina Rybacek, who copyedited the final draft in a very skillful manner. Mary Ann Buckles and Elizabeth Burford typed different portions with unusual dedication. Once Mary Ann spent the whole night trying to get the tables right. Elizabeth typed most of the first draft and the revisions, with her characteristic competence and good humor in the face of deadlines. My wife Susana and daughter Anna showed tolerance.

December 1986

Reversal of Development in Argentina

1 The Argentine Riddle and Sociology of Development

A story is told about a conversation between two diplomats in Buenos Aires. Says the first: "This country is a riddle to me. I have been here five months and I can't understand what is going on." Says the other: "Congratulations! You have a very keen apperception. I have been here for five years and have just reached the same conclusion."

—Felix J. Weil, *The Argentine Riddle*

The failure of Argentina . . . is one of the mysteries of our time.

—V.S. Naipaul, *The Return of Eva Perón*

The Argentine Question

The economic and political development of Argentina for the past one hundred years raises what in nineteenth-century language would have been called "a question": the failure of the country to become an industrial democracy. As with the other "questions"—peasant, national, etc.—the issue here is an apparent anomaly, an encounter with stubborn facts that challenge preexisting generalizations. And this anomaly is significant enough to become a problem for theory: in this instance, an opportunity to extend the theory of development in order to encompass what appears as a deviant case.

Argentine reality in the past decades—stagnation and hyperinflation in the economy, authoritarianism and praetorianism in the polity—may appear "natural" to the casual observer, who is likely to lump Argentina together with other countries into a stereotype called "Latin America," a kind of society in which these traits are normal and therefore expected. A more sophisticated reader might argue that what I am calling the "Argentine question" is a pseudoproblem: the issue of why some countries develop economically and politically while others do not is certainly valid, but I would be asking the question from the wrong perspective. In the tradition of Weber and Parsons, the problem is to understand the specific characteristics of the few countries that have established advanced capitalist economies and stable liberal democracies, for these are the deviant cases. It is the understanding of their peculiarities that would enable us to explain why all the other nations, Argentina included, have remained in the periphery or semi-periphery of the world system.

Argentine development, however, has puzzled observers and scholars for several decades now. Familiar comments made by economists (Simon Kuznetz used to say that there were two countries whose evolution could not be understood by economic theory: Japan and Argentina, while W. Arthur Lewis characterized Argentina as "strikingly backward in relation to its relative riches"[1]) reflect the perspective from which the Argentine question is pertinent: Argentina, as a society rich in resources and with a population mostly made up of European immigrants who settled there in the late nineteenth and early twentieth centuries, resembles the "new countries" or "lands of recent settlement," such as Australia, Canada, New Zealand, and the United States. There is a long tradition in economic and social thought, from Adam Smith to the staple theory of growth, which hypothesizes that these societies will evolve along the lines of dynamic capitalism and stable liberal democracy. The development of these nations—and also of Argentina, up to the Depression—bears out these expectations. It is, then, in relation to these "new countries" that Argentina appears as a deviant case. The contrast with Australia or New Zealand seems especially relevant, for Argentina shared with these nations, until the Depression, the position of supplier of grains, beef, and wool to Europe, and especially to Britain.

The Argentine case is also baffling for an empirical reason: the country's economic and political development has been curvilinear. The century 1880–1980 can be divided into two halves, whose characteristics are sharply different. Up to the Depression, Argentina was both a fast-growing economy and an expanding and rela-

---

1. A reference to statements of this type seems to be *de rigueur* in a book on Argentine development. I do not know if there is a written source for Kuznets's often quoted assertion, but I heard it from Kuznets himself at a seminar in the early seventies. As for Lewis's quotation, it is from W. Arthur Lewis, *Growth and Fluctuations, 1870–1913* (1978), p. 223. A list of the Argentines who have addressed the "Argentine question" would be very long. It would include authors I cite in this chapter, such as Federico Pinedo, Raúl Prebisch, and Carlos Escudé (who begins his recent book by posing the "question" in a manner quite similar to mine), and most of the many I discuss in Chapter 3. If the "question" is understood in the most general terms, as an inquiry into what is wrong—or went wrong—with Argentina, then it has been a remarkably persistent point of departure for all kinds of empirical analyses and ideological statements, beginning with mid-nineteenth century intellectuals and politicians such as Juan B. Alberdi, Esteban Echeverría, and Domingo F. Sarmiento. It is indeed noteworthy that, practically since the formation of the nation, authors with different ideologies and agendas have approached Argentina with the premise that something was wrong with it; that is, that the country's actual reality departed from what could be potentially expected on the basis of its natural, social, or cultural characteristics.

tively stable liberal democracy. The political crisis appeared in 1930, when the establishment of a military regime interrupted almost seventy years of constitutional legality and the economic crisis became evident around 1950, when stagnating tendencies emerged. There was, then, a reversal of economic and political development, and the period between the Depression and the end of World War II was the watershed.

In the second half of the nineteenth century, Argentina was fully incorporated into the international division of labor as an exporter of temperate agricultural commodities. The period from the seventies up to the Depression was one of rapid economic and social change. The population was 1.7 million in 1869, but from 1870 to 1930 it was engulfed by over six million European immigrants, over half of whom eventually remained in the country. At the end of the century, Argentina had attained a relatively high level of economic development: "As early as 1895, according to Michael M. Mulhall, the Argentine per capita income was about the same as those of Germany, Holland, and Belgium, and higher than those of Austria, Spain, Italy, Switzerland, Sweden, and Norway."[2] And Lewis writes that Argentine exports grew "at an average rate of 6 percent per annum, making Argentina compete with Japan for the title of the fastest growing country in the world between 1870 and 1913."[3] From the beginning of the century up to the Depression, the GDP grew at a rate of 4.6 percent per annum.[4]

World War I was the first major crisis of the international division of labor since the "big depression" of 1873, and after it the Argentine economy slowed down: whereas, during the years 1900–14, the GDP grew by 6.3 percent per annum, the rate fell to 3.5 percent during the years 1914–29. In comparison with other countries, as indicated in Table 1.1, Argentina's per capita GDP at the outbreak of World War I was almost equal to Switzerland's and higher than Sweden's or France's.[5] When the Depression hit, and

2. Carlos F. Díaz Alejandro, *Essays on the Economic History of the Argentine Republic* (1970), p. 1n.

3. Lewis, *Growth and Fluctuations*, p. 197.

4. United Nations, *El desarrollo económico de la Argentina* (1959), vol. 1, p. 15.

5. For longitudinal comparisons of per capita product involving either more countries or more points in time than those presented in Table 1.1, see Alfred Maizels, *Industrial Growth and World Trade* (1963), p. 533; World Bank, *Trends in Developing Countries* (1971), chap. 3; and Carlos Escudé, *Gran Bretaña, Estados Unidos y la declinación*

Table 1.1.
Ratios of the Argentine per Capita Product to that of Other Selected Countries, 1913–82.

Country	1913[1]	1929[1]	1937[1]	1957[1]	1965[2]	1978[3]	1982[4]
Canada	.48	.52	.57	.38	.31	.21	.22
Australia	.49	.49	.47	.41	.38	.24	.23
Britain	.51	.59	.48	.47	.42	.38	.26
Switzerland	.99	.75	.72	.49	.33	.16	.15
Sweden	1.09	.82	.61	.43	.30	.19	.18
France	1.18	.89	.94	.60	.40	.23	.22
Austria	1.38	1.42	1.38	.88	.60	.27	.26
Italy	2.09	1.96	1.96	1.16	.70	.50	.37
Japan	7.23	3.72	2.76	2.75	.89	.26	.25
Chile	—	2.20	1.34	1.92	1.36	1.35	1.14
Mexico	—	—	2.22	2.37	1.69	1.48	1.11
Brazil	—	5.14	3.52	2.47	2.88	1.22	1.13
(Argentina)	(470)	(540)	(510)	(605)	(770)	(1,910)	(2,520)

[1] Per capita GDP in 1955 U.S. dollars. Computed on the basis of Alfred Maizels, *Industrial Growth and World Trade* (Cambridge: Cambridge University Press, 1963).

[2] Per capita GNP in 1965 U.S. dollars. Computed on the basis of Charles L. Taylor and Michael C. Hudson, *World Handbook of Political and Social Indicators*, 2nd ed. (New Haven: Yale University Press, 1972).

[3] Per capita GNP in 1978 U.S. dollars. Computed on the basis of World Bank, *Poverty and Human Development* (New York: Oxford University Press, 1980).

[4] Per capita GNP in 1982 U.S. dollars. Computed n the basis of World Bank, *World Development Report* (New York: Oxford University Press, 1984).

in spite of the postwar slowdown, the GDP was still much higher than those of Austria or Italy.

The economy not only grew, but it also diversified. Manufacturing, which began in the late nineteenth century as a forward linkage of agriculture, expanded in the twenties on the basis of foreign investment, and in the thirties and forties as a consequence of the automatic protection that followed the Depression and the war. Around 1940, the contributions of manufacturing and agriculture to the GDP were comparable,[6] and in the early forties the labor

---

argentina, 1942–1949 (1983), pp. 17 and 370. For the period 1899–1957, both the World Bank and Escudé rely on Maizels's estimates.

6. Estimates of the Central Bank of the Argentine Republic, in the statistical appendix of Díaz Alejandro, *Essays*, p. 415.

force in the secondary sector was larger than the one in the primary sector.[7] In the mid-forties, the proportion of the population living in cities over 100,000 was higher than in the United States and most of Europe.[8]

Economic growth and diversification allowed a relatively high standard of living. At the outbreak of the Depression, indicators of nutrition, health, consumption, and access to higher education placed Argentina ahead of most of Europe. It is not easy to reconcile the image of Argentina as a typical Latin American society with facts such as that, at the time of the Depression, it ranked ahead of Britain in per capita number of automotive vehicles,[9] or that at the beginning of World War II, it had more physicians per capita than any country in Europe except Switzerland and Hungary.[10] Colin Clark included Argentina among the countries with the highest standards of living in 1925–34, together with the United States, Britain, the British dominions, and Switzerland.[11]

Before the turning point, the political system can be characterized as an expanding elite democracy. Pluralism and, more specifically, toleration of peaceful opposition existed, but participation was severely restricted by the electoral practices and the large proportion of foreigners, a negligible proportion of whom adopted Argentine citizenship. Power was monopolized by the landed elite, labeled "the oligarchy" by its opponents, but pressures for participation by the large middle class led to an electoral reform that established secret and universal manhood suffrage—but only for natives, it should be remembered. At the time of World War I, power was peacefully transferred to the opposition Radicals, who represented a heterogeneous constituency with a large middle class component.

A prominent member of that oligarchy, former finance minister Federico Pinedo, melancholically surveyed the Argentina of the Centennial (1910) from the vantage point of the turmoil of the sixties and described the political system thus:

7. The secondary sector includes manufacturing, construction, transport, and utilities. United Nations, *El desarrollo económico*, vol. 1, p. 37.

8. W. S. Woytinsky and E. S. Woytinsky, *World Population and Production: Trends and Outlook* (1953), p. 117.

9. Comité Nacional de Geografía, *Anuario geográfico argentino* (1941), cited by Díaz Alejandro, *Essays*, p. 56.

10. Woytinsky and Woytinsky, *Population and Production*, p. 229.

11. Colin Clark, *The Conditions of Economic Progress* (1940), p. 2.

... [the country] ... had already "taken off" and surged, accompanying the wealthiest and most progressive peoples in their triumphal march. Already, no one would have considered it among the backward countries, euphemistically called "underdeveloped" half a century later[12]. ... We had the characteristics of a well-ordered nation, prone to peaceful evolution and to the gradual overcoming of difficulties. One could argue about the degree of reality of our republican-representative institutions, but ... at least in respect to civil life, the fundamental institutions characteristic of the most civilized and prosperous nations of that time reigned here. ... It is good to remember ... that a period of sixty or seventy years of continuous political peace and regular succession of governments since the middle of the last century was not had by the United States, which underwent in this period the tragedy of the war of secession. It was not had by France, which saw in that lapse of time the fall of the "censitaire" monarchy, the birth and crumbling of the Second Republic, the appearance, apogee, and fall of the authoritarian [Second] Empire ... and attended the turbulent awakening of the Third Republic. It was not had by Spain, which saw its monarchy fall and rebound; neither Italy knew it, nor the Germanic world, which went through bloody convulsions and tearings before reaching national unity. Not even the quiet Swiss enjoyed it completely. ...[13]

The situation after the Depression and World War II has been a sharp reversal. Standards of living continued to be relatively high, as indicated for instance by the fact that life expectancy in the late seventies was still in the same range as in the United States and Europe,[14] or that enrollment in higher education was higher in the mid-sixties than in any European nation except the Netherlands.[15] But well-being was deteriorating or remaining stagnant in many areas, while European and other Latin American countries continued improving theirs.

12. Federico Pinedo, *Siglo y medio de economía argentina* (1961), p. 70.

13. Ibid., pp. 16–17.

14. World Bank, *Poverty and Human Development* (1980), pp. 68–69.

15. Charles L. Taylor and Michael C. Hudson, *World Handbook of Political and Social Indicators* (1972), pp. 229–31.

Steady economic growth came to a halt after a spectacular up-surge immediately after World War II. The per capita GDP grew at an annual rate of only 0.9 percent in the fifties, jumped to 2.8 per-cent in the sixties and 2.3 percent in the first half of the seventies, fell to almost zero (0.3 percent) during the rest of the decade, and was negative in the early eighties.[16] Argentina was not literally stagnant after World War II, but its economy was characterized by sharp fluctuations—stop-go cycles—so that "good" and "bad" years almost cancelled each other out. The growth rate of the per capita GDP in the period 1950–83 was about 1 percent. The signif-icance of this sluggishness is apparent when the Argentine per-formance is compared to that of other nations. Argentina slipped: its development, as measured by per capita product, is now closer to Latin American levels than it is to European or those of "new" countries. If in 1913, as Table 1.1 shows, Argentine per capita product was comparable to that of Switzerland, twice as large as that of Italy, and almost half that of Canada, in 1978 the corre-sponding proportions were less than one sixth, half, and one fifth. The contrast with Japan, the other country whose development economic theory could not understand, is dramatic: the Argentine per capita product, which was over five times that of Japan around World War I, and almost three times larger in the late fifties, was just one fourth in the early eighties. Further, the gap that separated Argentina from Brazil or Mexico in the late fifties was reduced by half in the late seventies.

The political transformation has been total. From 1930 to the coming to power of the constitutional government in 1983, Argen-tina wavered between authoritarian or exclusionary regimes and populist-corporatist ones, all highly unstable. Between 1930 and 1980, there were five major military coups (1943, 1955, 1962, 1966, and 1976), and countless minor ones. There were twenty-two presidents in this period, one of whom (Perón) was in power for about ten years. As for the nature of the deviation from liberal democracy, there were in this period nineteen years of military rule (1930–32, 1943–46, 1955–58, 1966–73, and 1976–80), thirteen years of Peronism, a regime with a populist-corporatist ideology, and nineteen years of restrictive democracy (1932–43 and 1958–66), an intermediate type that preserved constitutional forms but banned the majority parties (the Radicals in the thirties and the

---

16. United Nations, ECLA, *Statistical Yearbook for Latin America, 1984* (1985), p. 146.

Peronists in the sixties). In the second half of the period (1955–80), political instability reached critical levels. There were then fourteen presidents, and all the elected ones were overthrown, except for one, Perón, who died after being in office for less than a year. Moreover, urban terrorism broke out in the seventies, and it triggered massive state terrorism.

The awareness of the downfall from the ranks of the rich to those of the poor came slowly to the Argentines, and the response was one of pain. Pinedo himself reacted in this way to the realization that Argentina was not a founding member of the OECD:

> A few months ago, when a certain institution was founded that was devoted to aiding underdeveloped nations and engaged in having those with the highest standards of living contribute to raising the conditions of the unfortunate peoples, the Argentine Republic was not placed among the countries in a position to help, but among the peoples that needed help. Among the countries deemed capable of giving aid we find not only little Denmark, a seller of meat and butter, but also others with a predominantly rural production and a makeup similar to ours, such as Australia, New Zealand, and South Africa. We also find, among those who must help to improve the life conditions of countries with as little fortune as ours, the great European people out of which in the course of the years came more than a million of its children. They came to this soil in search of a better standard of living than their fatherland could give them. This is a humiliating aberration.[17]

This pattern of reversal raises the question about Argentina's failure to become an industrial democracy. Economic sluggishness and the breakdown of the liberal regime are, as can be suspected and as we will see in later chapters, causally interrelated. "Argentine exceptionalism" does not reside in the economic or in the political evolution of the country, but in the peculiar interaction between economy and polity. Before 1930, the two had a functional relationship: economic expansion made an expanding liberal democracy possible, and political stability contributed to economic growth. After World War II, however, the relationship

17. Pinedo, *Economía argentina*, pp. 21–22.

between economy and polity is such that economic languidness and instability trigger political instability, and this in turn contributes to the worsening of the economic crisis.

The problem is: why has Argentina been incapable of coupling an industrial society with liberal democracy? Even if the predictions based on the inclusion of the country among the lands of recent settlement are discarded, the problem is still puzzling, for Argentina, in the postwar period, had many of the prerequisites for liberal democracy postulated by different theories. It had no feudal past nor a precapitalist peasantry. Also, it had a population with a relatively high level of cultural and religious homogeneity, a high level of urbanization, a large manufacturing sector, central productive resources largely controlled by domestic groups, a large middle class, relatively high levels of education, well-established and highly organized interest groups and political parties, and it lacked a mass radical Left.

Some of the most obvious explanatory factors that come to mind, such as culture or dependency, do not, at first sight, appear adequate. Supporters of the proposition that Argentine development differs from that of the lands of recent settlement because the Latin-Mediterranean population, unlike the Anglo-Saxon one, is not prone to dynamic capitalism or to liberal democracy, would have to grapple with the fact of discontinuity. Since culture changes slowly, it cannot explain a sharp reversal of economic and political evolution. As for dependency or imperialism, it cannot be argued that the outcomes under discussion are the result of foreign domination, for, as we shall see, Argentine dependency decreased rather than increased when the economic and political decline took place.

These and other factors that have been advanced as an explanation, or that appear at first sight as plausible explanations, yield little when confronted with the facts. And the provisional answer to the riddle, which I am inclined to accept—that the reversal was caused by the unintended consequences of a specific set of policies adopted in the forties—opens an inquiry rather than closes it, for it will take us into the territory of elite rationality. I will argue that the decline of Argentina was the result of policies with which sectors of the elite believed they were protecting their interests. More specifically, they sacrificed economic growth for what they thought were their long-term political interests, and they produced a situation in which the latter were clearly endangered.

The Breakdown of the International Order and Its Consequences

It should be clear that the reversal of development in Argentina was not just the local repercussion of processes taking place in the world system between the Depression and the war.

The Argentine turning point cannot be considered in isolation, especially when we realize that this turning point coincided with a radical transformation in the nature of the world system into which Argentina was fully integrated. Structural determination appears overwhelming at first sight, but even casual observation suffices to lay aside the hypothesis of an automatic and direct link between structural changes at the world level and domestic discontinuities. Even though there is some commonality in the way in which different countries were affected by the Depression and the war, the variety of responses is such that only one conclusion is warranted: the relationship between world system transformation and local effects is mediated by the specific characteristics of each society.

Those historians who are fond of labeling centuries will not have a difficult time with ours. Looking at the twentieth century from the vantage point of our present time, it is clear that its dominant theme is the pursuit of a new equilibrium. The nineteen hundreds are characterized by the breakdown, with the Depression, of the economic and political order that came into being in the second half of the previous century and by the subsequent search for a new balance, whose contours have been taking shape since the end of World War II.

World War I was the first jolt to the preexisting order, but the system regained its equilibrium—with the loss of Russia, which broke away from the capitalist economy. It is in the period between 1930 and 1945 that the economic and political order was transformed. The significance of that period as a watershed becomes clearer when it is compared with the three or four decades that preceded and that followed it. These seminal fifteen years saw the structuring and consolidation of Stalinism and the formation of the Soviet Union we know today, the apogee of fascism in Italy, the end of Weimar and the establishment of nazism in Germany, the New Deal in the United States, the Popular Front and the collapse of the Third Republic in France, the Popular Front, the Civil War, and the emergence of the first modern authoritarian regime in Spain, the development of the welfare state in several West European countries, the inception of the Soviet bloc in Eastern Europe, the consolidation of the cleavages in China that would lead to Mao's victory, the expansion and collapse of Japan, the military regimes in many Latin American countries, the appearance of corporatism in Argentina and Brazil, the growth of nationalism in regions of Asia and Africa. . . . These are the events that shaped the world as the generations living today know it.

To a large extent, changes occurring after World War II are no more than the extension or deepening of transformations that began in 1930–45. This is clear in the cases in which the linkage is explicit—for example, the expansion of communism to countries such as Cuba or Afghanistan—but there are less explicit bonds, which, in many cases, are hidden to the actors and to most observers. Fascism is a case in point: *strictu sensu* there were only two cases, Italy and Germany, but the term is applied, in an ideological manner, to postwar authoritarian regimes such as that of Franco in Spain and of Pinochet in Chile. This usage is only understandable in the diffuse world of practical politics, for the regimes in question—and their many equivalents in the Latin American world— lack the central institutional and ideological components of fascism: a highly mobilized polity, under the control of a mass party that centralizes power; a nationalist ideology that presents itself not as reactionary but as revolutionary, not only as anticommunist but also as anticapitalist and, more specifically, antibourgeois; and a relatively high level of legitimacy (after opponents to the regime were excluded from the political community).[18]

These institutional and ideological traits are totally absent in contemporary authoritarian regimes, which are low-participation polities with some relatively independent interest groups, but usually with no political parties allowed, with inarticulate varieties of anticommunism and antiliberalism as an ideology, and with very low levels of legitimacy. But the components of fascism are alive and well in Asia and Africa, where countless "revolutionary" and "democratic" (and some of them also "popular") polities combine mobilizational traits, high centralization, a single party—*de jure* or *de facto*—and a nationalist noncommunist but anticapitalist ideology. I am not suggesting, of course, that these

18. See Juan J. Linz, "Some Notes Toward a Comparative Study of Fascism in Sociological Historical Perspective," in Walter Lacqueur, ed., *Fascism: A Reader's Guide* (1976), pp. 3–121; Ernst Nolte, *Three Faces of Fascism* (1965); A. James Gregor, *The Fascist Persuasion in Radical Politics* (1974).

third world regimes also have, or may develop, the most gruesome aspects of classical fascism. I am only indicating that what appears as a discontinuity in the world system is to a large extent a resonance of processes that reached their climax in the seminal interwar period. Traits that evolved in the polities of the "have nots" of the center at that time reemerge now in much of the periphery, and many times under the banner of "antifascism."

But let us go back to the economic and political order that existed between the two "big depressions" of the 1870s and the 1930s and to the position of Argentina in that system. Argentine politicians and government officials of all political stripes were well aware that the rapid growth of their economy and the consequent transformation of their society were the reflex of a dynamic impulse coming from Europe. Well before dependency theory and the world system approach became fashionable, and not likely having read Rosa Luxemburg and the theorists of imperialism, they conceptualized the international division of labor in terms of center and periphery—these very terms would be the focus of Raúl Prebisch's work since the late forties.[19] Further, they were equally aware of the fact that there were different types of periphery and that Argentina belonged to a category more economically and socially advanced than others, to what Immanuel Wallerstein calls the semiperiphery.

The distinctive traits of that international order are well known. In the economy, the basic norm was the relatively unrestrained mobility of commodities, capital, and labor between the countries in the center, among which Britain was the dominant power, and between center and periphery. Argentine development after the depression of 1873 was reactive, and also externally induced. Not only European industrialization and urbanization provided a demand for temperate agricultural commodities, but Britain and other European countries supplied the capital for railroads and meat-packing houses, and Italy and Spain provided the workers. It was the peculiar structure of the international economy that allowed the relatively unimpeded circulation of these inputs.

In the society, the basic process was the generalization of capitalist social relations, that is, of production on the basis of labor markets, up to the point where these relations tended to become

19. See Raúl Prebisch, *The Economic Development of Latin America and Its Principal Problems* (1950). On the doctrine of the Economic Commission for Latin America of the United Nations, see Octavio Rodríguez, *La teoría del subdesarrollo de la CEPAL* (1980).

exclusive in the center and in the most advanced countries of the periphery, Argentina being one of the latter. In the remainder of the periphery, incorporation into the world economy brought about structural heterogeneity: the separation between workers and the land or the instruments of labor in the "modern" sector and, in the rest of society, the preservation or re-creation of traditional social relations, be they feudal or communitarian, which existed before the development of capitalism or were produced by its previous stages. Argentina and Uruguay in Latin America, and the lands of recent settlement elsewhere, were probably the only noncore countries in which production based on free labor was prevalent at the end of the nineteenth century. In the Argentine case, traditional social relations, mainly subsistence agriculture, existed, but were gradually absorbed. The large-scale inflow of traditional populations into the labor markets of the domestic center, however, did not occur until the thirties and forties, when the Depression produced an agrarian crisis and import-substituting industrialization developed.

In the polity, the distinctive trait of the period was the diffusion of liberalism in the center and in the most advanced sectors of the periphery, Argentina included. The two dimensions of liberal democracy, pluralism or toleration of dissent, and participation,[20] had an uneven degree of institutionalization. The first one became established in all countries of the center—including authoritarian regimes such as Imperial Germany—and in much of the periphery, not only in the areas where capitalist social relations prevailed, such as Argentina, but also in many structurally heterogeneous societies in Latin America. (Some limited forms of toleration of dissent were even appearing in Russia toward the end of the czarist regime.) The second dimension, participation, was significantly institutionalized only in some countries of the center—even though suffrage was nowhere "universal"—but in sectors of the periphery, Argentina included, there was a clear trend toward the enfranchisement of the middle and lower classes. Peace among nations, finally, was maintained by balance of power policies.

This is the order that began to crumble with World War I and its consequences—the Russian revolution, Italian fascism, the collapse of the German Empire—which were the seeds of World War II. But the watershed, especially in the non-European world, was

20. See Robert A. Dahl, *Polyarchy: Participation and Opposition* (1971), chap. 1.

the Depression: it was after 1930 that the rules of the economic and political game were transformed. In the economy, international trade broke down, protection and bilateralism appeared everywhere, international transfers of capital declined, and the immigration flow stopped. In the polity, the "night watchman" state disappeared, and liberal democracies began to develop their welfare states. But the most distinctive change was the expansion of nondemocratic kinds of state, including not only the totalitarian cases but also the authoritarian forms that flourished in southern and eastern Europe and in much of Latin America. The war, finally, destroyed, even for Argentina and other countries not directly involved in the conflict, any semblance of an ordered international system, any hope that the same equilibrium that existed prior to the Depression could be reestablished. And uncertainty about the future shape of the world order was total, especially in the early forties, when a victory by the Axis seemed a strong possibility.

After the war, a new international system began to emerge, with new participants and slowly evolving new norms for their economic and political interaction. The structural changes each country had experienced during the almost two decades of disequilibrium would determine its position in the new arrangement. Since most of the less developed countries in Latin America had experienced little structural changes, their reinsertion was not difficult. Thus, in the postwar international economic and political system these societies occupied positions that differed very little from those they had prior to 1930 (*vide* most Central American countries). It was the middle developed nations such as Argentina, and the highly developed ones, which had changed basic aspects of their economy and society. For them, adaptation into the new order was problematic: their role would depend on the degree of fit between their new structural characteristics and the evolving traits of the international system.

And some countries had changed radically. The patterns of domestic economic and political discontinuity associated with the transformation of the international system between 1930 and 1945 vary in such a way that the hypothesis of direct and exclusive structural causation has to be rejected: previous position in the system is not a predictor of the type of response. André G. Frank's popular argument about the economic consequences of the relaxation or rupture of linkages between a country and the interna-

the threat of revolution. This plausible hypothesis, which figured prominently in Marxist analyses of fascism, is usually emphasized in the discussion of authoritarianism as well.

A Marxist structural framework of this classical type can illuminate important aspects of the Argentine case, such as the differences between Argentina and the Latin American model, the impact of the world economy, and the effects of interclass relations, but it is inadequate to explain the peculiar pattern of this country's economic and political development, for two reasons. First, Argentina is not "dualistic" or structurally heterogeneous, at least as far as feudal or traditional-communitarian survivals are concerned: the social structure is homogeneously capitalist. Second, the breakdown of liberal democracy has not been a ruling-class response to a threat of revolution from below. This does not mean that working class mobilization has been absent: there have been periods of rather militant collective action, and their consequences have been destabilizing, but there was not a realistic menace of revolution at the time of the reversal.

Classical functionalism is even less appropriate as a tool for the understanding of the Argentine pattern. It is true that functionalist theorists have been aware of the contingent nature of the links between environmental changes and the differentiation of a system, between differentiation and integration within a system, and between these internal changes and an enhanced adaptation to the environment. These contingencies can be discerned, even if sometimes only implicitly, in Parsons' conceptualization of evolutionary change in terms of four mechanisms—differentiation, integration, inclusion, and value generalization[29]—and they are more clear in Neil Smelser's analysis of the counterpoint between differentiation and integration, and of the consequences of lags between them.[30] Shmuel Eisenstadt, finally, has discussed the "roads not taken" in a systematic manner, in terms of breakdowns of modernization leading to stagnation or retrogression.[31]

29. See Talcott Parsons, *Societies: Evolutionary and Comparative Perspectives* (1966), *The System of Modern Societies* (1971), and "Comparative Studies and Evolutionary Change," in Ivan Vallier, ed., *Comparative Methods in Sociology* (1971).

30. See the classical discussion in Neil J. Smelser, "Mechanisms of Change and Adjustment to Change," in Bert F. Hoselitz and Wilbert E. Moore, eds., *Industrialization and Society* (1966), and also Smelser, *Social Change in the Industrial Revolution* (1959).

31. See S. N. Eisenstadt, "Social Change, Differentiation, and

tional system—he classified the effects into "active" and "passive" involution,[21] that is, growth or decline—can be extended to the political realm, as a cursory review of the variance of responses shows. This is obvious in relation to core countries—see the development of the welfare state in the United States or Sweden, versus the installation of nazism in Germany or the sequence of the Popular Front and Vichy in France—but is also true in the periphery. In Latin America, the thirties and forties correspond to authoritarian regimes and corporatist experiments in Argentina and Brazil, the Popular Front government in Chile, and movement toward the left in Mexico under Cárdenas. Among "lands of recent settlement," finally, the Argentine experience differs from that of the other countries in the group.

At a very general level, it is possible to argue that, beyond institutional differences, there is a common aspect of these and the other responses to the Depression and the war: the growth of the power and autonomy of the state vis-à-vis economic elites, interest groups, and political parties. But the differences in the degree of such a response—among, let us say, the welfare state in a liberal democracy, an authoritarian regime in a context of "limited pluralism," and the totalitarian state—are more important than this common element of centralization of power for the explanation of the subsequent evolution of the different societies.

The reversal of development in Argentina was not, then, just the local effect of the transformation of the world system between the Depression and the war. The international position of Argentina as an exporter of beef and grains and an importer of manufactures and investment capital, and as a participant in Britain's informal empire interacted with other, that is, "internal" characteristics of the society—such as its institutional structure or the objective and cultural traits of its constituent groups—to "produce" a sluggish and unstable economy and deviation from liberal democracy.[22] The key to the understanding of the differences between Argentina and other countries that occupied a similar position in the international economy and that, up to 1930–45, had comparable patterns of evolution is to be found in that social black box.

21. André G. Frank, *Capitalism and Underdevelopment in Latin America* (1969).

22. A similar point is made by Tony Smith in his *The Pattern of Imperialism* (1981).

Argentina and Social Theory

The analysis of the Argentine case is relevant for a central issue in sociology of development: the need to develop a theory that transcends the old unilinear models and the more recent comparisons between typical patterns and that is also capable of encompassing the cases of "failure"—with respect to a theoretical model—in any of its forms: malformation, stagnation, retrogression.

The significance of this case for development theory is heightened by the fact that Argentine evolution is paradoxical in relation to the classical versions of Marxism and functionalism, the two major frameworks that, in pure or mixed forms, are still the foundation of the sociological analysis of development. The deterministic varieties of Marxism in circulation do not seem adequate to explain the economic slippage and the propensity for nondemocratic forms of state in a society such as Argentina, in which the capitalist mode of production is almost exclusive and in which there is not a high level of class polarization. Furthermore, functionalist models of Parsonian inspiration lack a theory for the explanation of the Argentine process of differentiation. It was triggered by environmental changes, which led to a type of integration, the objective consequence of which was a decrease in the level of adaptation.

It is clear that the leading Marxist writers have always been sensitive at the empirical level to the differential economic performance of capitalist societies and to the fact that some capitalist economies do not give rise to liberal-democratic polities. Marx himself noted the differences between French capitalism and the English model,[23] and both Marx and Engels carried out a remarkable analysis of Germany, showing how the persistence of the Junkers as a fraction of the ruling class distorted both the economic and the political evolution of that country, and led to the formation of a nondemocratic state.[24] Later, Lenin, Bukharin, and Rosa Luxemburg introduced the structure of the world economy as a central factor in explaining the differential economic performance—and, indirectly, the political as well—of societies. Their analysis, however, with the exception of Luxemburg's, focuses on

23. See Karl Marx, *The Class Struggles in France (1848–1850)* (1972), p. 113.

24. See Friedrich Engels, *The German Revolutions* (1967), and *The Role of Force in History: A Study of Bismarck's Policy of Blood and Iron* (1968).

processes in the center and disregards the causal weight of economic and political processes in the periphery—perhaps as a belated reflection of Hegel's (and possibly Marx's) belief that these are nations "without history."[25] Trotsky, finally, provided the first systematic analysis of structural heterogeneity in his discussion of Russia as a case of "combined" development, in which capitalist social relations are generated in such a way that the precapitalist ones persist.[26] Contemporary writers such as Paul Baran, Fernando H. Cardoso, André G. Frank, Osvaldo Sunkel and other dependency theorists, and Immanuel Wallerstein, have conceptually refined and empirically developed the analysis of different types of capitalist economy and the social and political consequences of different locations in the international division of labor.[27] Among modern structuralists, Nicos Poulantzas has focused his work on the relationship between capitalism and "states of exception," authoritarianism and fascism included.[28]

What can classical Marxism suggest about the reversal of Argentine development? Not much. In Marxism, economic stagnation and deviation from liberal democracy appear in two theoretical contexts. First, as correlates of "impure" capitalism, these are possible consequences of structural heterogeneity and/or a high level of external control. In the Marxist tradition, there has been a single model of capitalist development—that of England in the nineteenth century—and the tendency has been to consider cases which diverge from that type as deviations. The rich empirical observations about intercountry differences have not been integrated into a "multipath" theory of capitalist development except for the dichotomies based on "impurity" as the implicit criterion: capitalist-precapitalist or "combined," dominant-dependent, etc. Second, in a "pure" capitalist society, nondemocratic political outcomes have tended to appear as a response

25. On this point, see José Aricó, *Marx y América Latina* (198

26. See Leon Trotsky, *The History of the Russian Revolution*

27. See the influential works by Paul A. Baran, *The Political* of Growth (1957); Fernando H. Cardoso and Enzo Faletto, *De* and Development in Latin America (1979); Frank, *Capitalis* Underdevelopment; Osvaldo Sunkel and Pedro Paz, *El subo* latinoamericano y la teoría del desarrollo (1970); Immanu Wallerstein, *The Capitalist World-Economy* (1979), and *Th* World System: Capitalist Agriculture and the Origins of t World-Economy in the Sixteenth Century (1974).

28. Nicos Poulantzas, *Political Power and Social Classe* Fascism and Dictatorship (1974).

tional system—he classified the effects into "active" and "passive" involution,[21] that is, growth or decline—can be extended to the political realm, as a cursory review of the variance of responses shows. This is obvious in relation to core countries—see the development of the welfare state in the United States or Sweden, versus the installation of nazism in Germany or the sequence of the Popular Front and Vichy in France—but is also true in the periphery. In Latin America, the thirties and forties correspond to authoritarian regimes and corporatist experiments in Argentina and Brazil, the Popular Front government in Chile, and movement toward the left in Mexico under Cárdenas. Among "lands of recent settlement," finally, the Argentine experience differs from that of the other countries in the group.

At a very general level, it is possible to argue that, beyond institutional differences, there is a common aspect of these and the other responses to the Depression and the war: the growth of the power and autonomy of the state vis-à-vis economic elites, interest groups, and political parties. But the differences in the degree of such a response—among, let us say, the welfare state in a liberal democracy, an authoritarian regime in a context of "limited pluralism," and the totalitarian state—are more important than this common element of centralization of power for the explanation of the subsequent evolution of the different societies.

The reversal of development in Argentina was not, then, just the local effect of the transformation of the world system between the Depression and the war. The international position of Argentina as an exporter of beef and grains and an importer of manufactures and investment capital, and as a participant in Britain's informal empire interacted with other, that is, "internal" characteristics of the society—such as its institutional structure or the objective and cultural traits of its constituent groups—to "produce" a sluggish and unstable economy and deviation from liberal democracy.[22] The key to the understanding of the differences between Argentina and other countries that occupied a similar position in the international economy and that, up to 1930–45, had comparable patterns of evolution is to be found in that social black box.

21. André G. Frank, *Capitalism and Underdevelopment in Latin America* (1969).

22. A similar point is made by Tony Smith in his *The Pattern of Imperialism* (1981).

Argentina and Social Theory

The analysis of the Argentine case is relevant for a central issue in sociology of development: the need to develop a theory that transcends the old unilinear models and the more recent comparisons between typical patterns and that is also capable of encompassing the cases of "failure"—with respect to a theoretical model—in any of its forms: malformation, stagnation, retrogression.

The significance of this case for development theory is heightened by the fact that Argentine evolution is paradoxical in relation to the classical versions of Marxism and functionalism, the two major frameworks that, in pure or mixed forms, are still the foundation of the sociological analysis of development. The deterministic varieties of Marxism in circulation do not seem adequate to explain the economic slippage and the propensity for nondemocratic forms of state in a society such as Argentina, in which the capitalist mode of production is almost exclusive and in which there is not a high level of class polarization. Furthermore, functionalist models of Parsonian inspiration lack a theory for the explanation of the Argentine process of differentiation. It was triggered by environmental changes, which led to a type of integration, the objective consequence of which was a decrease in the level of adaptation.

It is clear that the leading Marxist writers have always been sensitive at the empirical level to the differential economic performance of capitalist societies and to the fact that some capitalist economies do not give rise to liberal-democratic polities. Marx himself noted the differences between French capitalism and the English model,[23] and both Marx and Engels carried out a remarkable analysis of Germany, showing how the persistence of the Junkers as a fraction of the ruling class distorted both the economic and the political evolution of that country, and led to the formation of a nondemocratic state.[24] Later, Lenin, Bukharin, and Rosa Luxemburg introduced the structure of the world economy as a central factor in explaining the differential economic performance—and, indirectly, the political as well—of societies. Their analysis, however, with the exception of Luxemburg's, focuses on

23. See Karl Marx, *The Class Struggles in France (1848–1850)* (1972), p. 113.

24. See Friedrich Engels, *The German Revolutions* (1967), and *The Role of Force in History: A Study of Bismarck's Policy of Blood and Iron* (1968).

processes in the center and disregards the causal weight of economic and political processes in the periphery—perhaps as a belated reflection of Hegel's (and possibly Marx's) belief that these are nations "without history."[25] Trotsky, finally, provided the first systematic analysis of structural heterogeneity in his discussion of Russia as a case of "combined" development, in which capitalist social relations are generated in such a way that the precapitalist ones persist.[26] Contemporary writers such as Paul Baran, Fernando H. Cardoso, André G. Frank, Osvaldo Sunkel and other dependency theorists, and Immanuel Wallerstein, have conceptually refined and empirically developed the analysis of different types of capitalist economy and the social and political consequences of different locations in the international division of labor.[27] Among modern structuralists, Nicos Poulantzas has focused his work on the relationship between capitalism and "states of exception," authoritarianism and fascism included.[28]

What can classical Marxism suggest about the reversal of Argentine development? Not much. In Marxism, economic stagnation and deviation from liberal democracy appear in two theoretical contexts. First, as correlates of "impure" capitalism, these are the possible consequences of structural heterogeneity and/or a high level of external control. In the Marxist tradition, there has been a single model of capitalist development—that of England in the nineteenth century—and the tendency has been to consider the cases which diverge from that type as deviations. The rich empirical observations about intercountry differences have not been integrated into a "multipath" theory of capitalist development, except for the dichotomies based on "impurity" as the implicit criterion: capitalist-precapitalist or "combined," dominant-dependent, etc. Second, in a "pure" capitalist society, nondemocratic political outcomes have tended to appear as a response to

25. On this point, see José Aricó, *Marx y América Latina* (1980).

26. See Leon Trotsky, *The History of the Russian Revolution* (1957).

27. See the influential works by Paul A. Baran, *The Political Economy of Growth* (1957); Fernando H. Cardoso and Enzo Faletto, *Dependency and Development in Latin America* (1979); Frank, *Capitalism and Underdevelopment*; Osvaldo Sunkel and Pedro Paz, *El subdesarrollo latinoamericano y la teoría del desarrollo* (1970); Immanuel Wallerstein, *The Capitalist World-Economy* (1979), and *The Modern World System: Capitalist Agriculture and the Origins of the European World-Economy in the Sixteenth Century* (1974).

28. Nicos Poulantzas, *Political Power and Social Classes* (1973), and *Fascism and Dictatorship* (1974).

the threat of revolution. This plausible hypothesis, which figured prominently in Marxist analyses of fascism, is usually emphasized in the discussion of authoritarianism as well.

A Marxist structural framework of this classical type can illuminate important aspects of the Argentine case, such as the differences between Argentina and the Latin American model, the impact of the world economy, and the effects of interclass relations, but it is inadequate to explain the peculiar pattern of this country's economic and political development, for two reasons. First, Argentina is not "dualistic" or structurally heterogeneous, at least as far as feudal or traditional-communitarian survivals are concerned: the social structure is homogeneously capitalist. Second, the breakdown of liberal democracy has not been a ruling-class response to a threat of revolution from below. This does not mean that working class mobilization has been absent: there have been periods of rather militant collective action, and their consequences have been destabilizing, but there was not a realistic menace of revolution at the time of the reversal.

Classical functionalism is even less appropriate as a tool for the understanding of the Argentine pattern. It is true that functionalist theorists have been aware of the contingent nature of the links between environmental changes and the differentiation of a system, between differentiation and integration within a system, and between these internal changes and an enhanced adaptation to the environment. These contingencies can be discerned, even if sometimes only implicitly, in Parsons' conceptualization of evolutionary change in terms of four mechanisms—differentiation, integration, inclusion, and value generalization[29]—and they are more clear in Neil Smelser's analysis of the counterpoint between differentiation and integration, and of the consequences of lags between them.[30] Shmuel Eisenstadt, finally, has discussed the "roads not taken" in a systematic manner, in terms of breakdowns of modernization leading to stagnation or retrogression.[31]

29. See Talcott Parsons, *Societies: Evolutionary and Comparative Perspectives* (1966), *The System of Modern Societies* (1971), and "Comparative Studies and Evolutionary Change," in Ivan Vallier, ed., *Comparative Methods in Sociology* (1971).

30. See the classical discussion in Neil J. Smelser, "Mechanisms of Change and Adjustment to Change," in Bert F. Hoselitz and Wilbert E. Moore, eds., *Industrialization and Society* (1966), and also Smelser, *Social Change in the Industrial Revolution* (1959).

31. See S. N. Eisenstadt, "Social Change, Differentiation, and